**Dear Sir or Madam Will Y
Took me Years to Write, Won**

Although now a flourishing part of the UK music scene, it has been suggested that Bolton's Buskers Ball was probably the very first open mic established some 40 years ago!

Indeed at one point it was included as an entry in the Encyclopedia Britannica's online edition, with an entry that read " a generic term for an informal gathering of acoustic based singers and musicians". I wrote to them, telling that it wasn't a generic term, but a specific term for 'open mics. that I was running in the Bolton area, a cross between a traditional folk club and a rock night... and they dutifully removed it.

Who knows if they hadn't, maybe there'd be Buskers Balls all over the place now!

The term 'Open Mic', came about when Canadian singer-songwriter Brent Mason heard about the Acoustic Sessions at Oscars (Bolton's premier music venue at the time, and still sadly missed) and suggested it.

Despite being pretty 'music savvy' I hadn't heard that term before, but thought it an apt description of what I was trying to achieve.

The aim of this book is twofold.

Firstly to give a very basic outline as to how it all started and how it developed. If I went into it in any more detail, this book would be so thick wouldn't fit on the shelves!

Secondly, to advise on starting and making a success of your open mic night. It is important to remember that it will be your night, and although the information in this book should prove very useful it's ultimately up to you how you want to run your sessions, and nothing is written in stone.

After doing it multiple times a week all over the country for over 40 years, to quote Rab Nesbitt:

"I think I've got the hang of it now"

The book itself came about when my son Jon recently started an open mic in a remote part of Scotland and asked for my advice on a the practicalities, equipment and do's and don'ts as there wasn't a good single source of information on the internet. After a while, I realised that I had given so much advice I could put it together to write half a book, so it only seemed logical to finish it off!

There are also quite a few photo's I've taken over the years which should show just how much things have changes (or not!).

If anybody has any photos from their early sessions, contact me and I may very well add them to a revised edition!

Alec Martin

The Times they were a Changing!

Alec Martin has earned a place as one on the founding fathers' of the British 'open mic' movement.

A member of The Beatles generation, his musical curiosity extended to artists such as Bert Jansch, Martin Carthy, The Incredible String Band, Woody Guthrie. Bob Dylan and a whole host of American country blues artists.

It was this style of music that steered him to buy a cheap acoustic guitar from Exchange & Mart, a guitar so flimsy it fell apart when his mother smashed it over his head when he neglected his school homework!
He was particularly grateful he hadn't chosen a solid body Gibson Les Paul!

The author at the age of 14 lazing around in garden

No doubt fueled by guilt, his mother quickly replaced it with a 'proper' guitar, an Eko Ranger 6, and armed with this, he edged into the heady world of folk music clubs which had begun to spring up all over the country, with a particularly large smattering in his native North West.

This was a bit of an eye opener to say the least!

Most of the folk clubs then (and indeed many today) ran along the lines of having pro guest nights interspersed every other week with 'singers nights' where less experienced musicians could indulge with their songs about Lord Franklyn, The Little Musgrave, and Streets of London.

Brownie points could be obtained if the song was credited with being 'traditional' or 'anon' about a subject so obscure it required a detailed history lesson before its actual performance.

In many cases the introduction was probably more interesting than the song itself, and, indeed, several pro singers developed the introduction to the point where it was actually longer than the song!

Mike Harding, Jasper Carrot, and Bob Williamson were some of the masters, and Billy Connolly refined the art to such an extent that he could virtually drop the songs all together!

These artists, that had learned their craft on the folk music circuit, became incredibly popular. One late night show on a particular Manchester radio station featured nothing but their 'music' and quite a few 'folk comedians' went on to get chart success.

Despite this however, the image of the folk club remained very dour to all but the true enthusiasts (but to be fair there were quite a lot of them).
No talking, no going to the bar or even the toilet whilst the artist was performing, and God help you if you knocked a glass off your table or struck a match to light a cigarette.! The atmosphere was pretty intense. Singing along with the chorus was encouraged though.

Some folk clubs dispensed with instruments completely, with the holding of what was known as 'Singarounds', where attendees would usually sit facing each other in a circle, taking turns to stand up and burst into song

These songs were of varying length but some could be more than a dozen verses. Add a dozen choruses where fellow members of the 'round' would eagerly join in, and songs could last 15 or 20 minutes!!!

Alec accidentally stumbled into a couple of these nights on his quest for his ideal music night, and they were excruciating to say the least.

Oh for someone to perform a Charlie Patton song or heaven forbid a Beatles tune!

A folk club in the late 60s, early 1970's

There is a House in Salford!

Around the early 1970's however, in the upstairs room of an unpromising, slightly dilapidated pub in Salford, he at last found a folk club he felt comfortable in.

The Black Lion, Salford

The Black Lion was run every Friday night by a no- nonsense kinda guy called Pete Farrow.

Pete was a truly larger than life character.

A one-man band operator who sat behind union jack truly draped bass drum, with a hi-hat, a plastic parrot affixed to one of the drum's attachments and usually wearing a battered top hat and sporting a jumbo sized guitar.

He didn't tolerate any talking whilst singers were performing... you'd get a verbal warning but if you repeated the offence, you'd be out!

The place got packed.

Full of quality musicians eager to play to an audience consisting of fellow troubadours, drunks, ladies of the night and true Manchester buskers, with a smattering of TV personalities and journalists who were working at Granada TV Studios just round the corner and Manchester's equivalent of Fleet St, Shudehill, just up the road. And just round the corner, a record stall that sold an amazing array of skiffle and blues records!

Alec thought 'Well this is alright!'

The atmosphere inside, thick with cigarette smoke, was electric, with a single white spotlight shining on the stage area, with the rest of the room in total darkness.

Although it started at 8pm, anybody wanting to perform really had to be there at least an hour earlier to ensure a spot, and even then you weren't guaranteed a place especially if Pete thought you were a bit wet between the ears.

Pete Farrow on the cover of one of the area's many magazines dedicated to the folk scene in the 1970s

Pete invariably kicked off the proceedings, playing a short set of country blues and jug-band stompers by the likes of Blind Blake and the Mississippi Sheiks, sometimes interspersing these tunes with one of his original ballad type songs.

After Pete came a succession of quality artists, too many to list (and many long since passed away). But stand out performances by Mary Asquith (Manchester's 'Queen of the Blues')
John Cooper Clarke, and Granada TV presenters Trevor Hyett and Anna Ford are etched in the annals.

Mary Asquith R.I.P.

Alec soaked up the atmosphere, and although he sometimes took his guitar (mainly to show everyone he was one of them) he doesn't remember actually daring to get up and play.

Come to think of it, he doesn't recall being asked. Maybe Pete thought him 'wet behind the ears' and maybe he was...

But the 18 months or so when he attended the Black Lion, left an indelible stamp.

This was what folk music was all about!

The author as a cool 1970's hipster

Despite doing the rounds of other folk clubs in the area (and even picking up a few paid gigs along the
way) Alec was determined to bring the Black Lion experience to his hometown of Bolton.

A couple of his friends suggested a pub that had been off his radar, The Victory on Chorley Old Road.

The Victory was one of Greenall's flagship boozers with heavy mahogany doors, lush carpets and was big. Best of all, it had a large concert room holding maybe
a couple of hundred people.

It was decided to call the night 'Cloggies' after the Bill Tidy cartoon column in Private Eye magazine which lampooned the folk scene, cocking a snoot at the other more traditional folk venues in the area.

Held every Sunday, Alec bedecked the tables with candles in wine bottles, a very bright white spotlight illuminating the stage (a nod to the Black Lion) and holy of holys a 100w Carlsbro PA system in situ, which belonged to the pub.

Opening night, Alec was expecting maybe a dozen people, but to his surprise it seemed like every musician in Bolton had turned up... it was jam packed.

The fake 'Hells Angels' on the door (who had appointed themselves as security) actually had to turn people away, although a bribe of a bottle of Newky brown ensured admittance!

Pete 'Bob Dylan' R.I.P a Cloggies regular, not only nailed the style and voice of 'the man' but also the attitue

The club lasted almost 3 years, a folk club with very little actual folk music.

The guest line-up week after week was very similar to that found at the Black Lion, and indeed Alec booked both Pete Farrow and Mary Asquith for regular guest spots.

Other visitors included Bob Williamson (who came to try out new material), Granada Reports presenters (who came expecting a tribute to Nelson Mandella when Alec mistakenly mis-spelled the name of his band called Mandala).

Ted Edwards (a traditional folkie who achieved national acclaim when he crossed the Sahara on a camel), Les Barker & Mrs Akroyd and John Cooper Clarke (turning up with Pete Farrow just before he hit the big time). We also had our resident magician Derek Austin, who enthralled the audience with his 'head cremation' trick ... with real flames!!

The most unusual act though was undoubtedly Ricker George whose debut involved him walking onstage with a box which everyone assumed to be an accordion, but when he opened it, it was an old 78rpm wind up gramophone which he used to play the Dambusters March, whilst playing the spoons grinning profusely!

Great stuff, but rather tedious after the first half a dozen times.

Ricker George came from Westhoughton but I have since heard there was another rival virtuoso living just a few miles away, by the name Ricker Joe!!

The Cakes, Bolton's answer to the Bonzo's and famous for their annual Xmas parties. Featured in the 50th anniversary edition of GQ magazine.

The Cakes went on to feature in the 50th anniversary edition of GQ magazine and were famous for their 'Beano Jig'

Pubs shut more or less bang on 10.30pm in those times of Sunday licensing (a time when modern day kids are just thinking of going out).

The fun-n-frolics didn't end then though.

After a swift visit to the newly opened KFC up the road, a few dozen people would head back to the derelict house behind The Victory, where the alleged 'Hells Angels' and their Alsatian dog 'Rebel' lived.

Fueled by the crates of brown ale the 'Angels' had bought with their illicit door charges, crazy parties went on until all hours.

At this point I must point out that although wearing 'colours', Bolton's outlaw bikers weren't actually the real deal.

Rumour has it, that a team of the real deal 'Angels' called at their house and put a shotgun through their door and the Bolton boys left town.

The after show parties ended after that!
One door opens and another closes though, and Alec's new friendship with Bob Williamson saw the pair go back to Bob's house after closing time, supping vodka and lime till the sun came up!

The reputation of Cloggies soon spread, resulting in Alec being asked to be one of the resident singers at the highly prestigious Poynton Folk Centre, where top of the bill were artists the calibre of Pete Seeger, Steeleye Span, Richard Thompson etc.

It was on Alec's watch that it was voted Folk Club of the Year in the main music weekly Melody Maker! Alec himself was invited to play the Manchester Evening News stage at the 25,000+ crowd Charnock Richard Folk Festival, with stars like Fairport Convention, Gallagher & Lyle, Country Joe, and interestingly enough, both Pete Farrow and Mary Asquith.

All things must pass however, and after around 3 years, the landlord of the Victory retired and it was decided to end Cloggies, with Alec drifting off the folk scene, going electric a la Bob Dylan, with his blues band Night Train, a band which still gigs regularly.

Alec always retained an interest in acoustic music however, and sporadically throughout the 80s held various acoustic nights in the Bolton area, but none achieved the success of his Cloggies venture, mainly due to the lack of suitable venues.

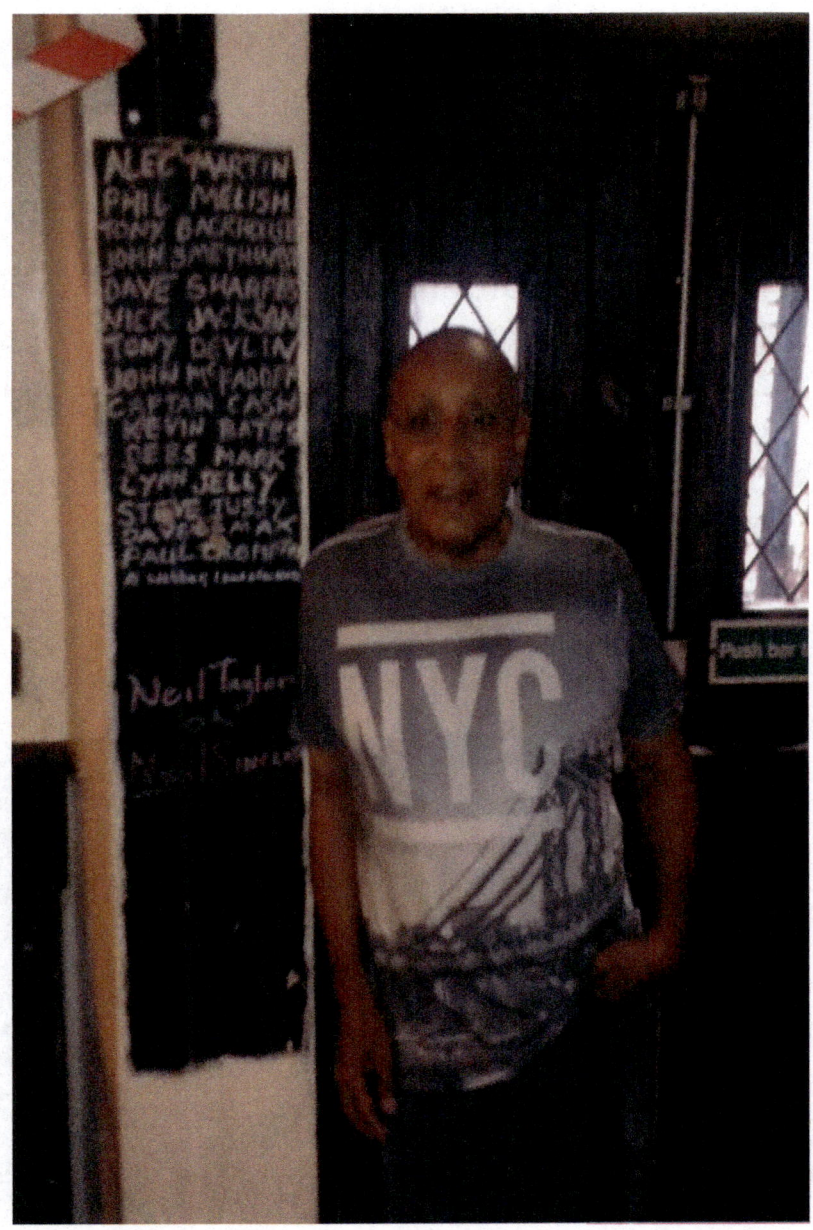

Permanent memorial to the musicians who played at John Jelly's wake at The Man & Schyte, Bolton.

In the early 90s though, Bolton's music scene was transformed with the opening of a new venue, Oscars.

A basement bar, Oscars owner, Gay Nuttall, was an avid music enthusiast, and whilst during the day she operated it as a cafe bar, in the evening it transformed into a five or six nights a week, full on music venue.
Separate nights were dedicated to new wave, punk, soul and various styles of rock.

Oscars entrance a sight familiar to many musicians. What lay beyond was a cruel two flight staircase, but when negotiated brought you into the best music venue in the north west.

One glaring omission however was acoustic music. In reality, it just wasn't as fashionable as it's more upbeat cousins.

Local music shops only carried a small selection of acoustic guitars, and folk music had largely been abandoned bar a few stalwart supporters.

Even the once supreme Poynton Folk Centre had gone in to what was to prove a terminal decline.

The only time Bolton people heard a singer with an acoustic guitar other than in their own homes, was a pair of buskers who frequented the town centre, swapping patches when they were asked to move on by the police.

One was a guy called Psychedelic Sid, and the other was Alec... and indeed it was these two, with the assistance of Bolton Trades Council, that got busking legalised in the town centre.

They were told if the police ever mistakenly tried to move them on, all they had to say was "judges rules" and that was it.

To this day nobody understands why!

Psychedelic Sid, Alec's busking partner in crime. Sid would start outside Bolton's C&A whilst Alec worked the Newport Arcade. If they got told to move, they'd simply change places.

Around a year after Oscars first opened, Alec floated the idea to Gay of an acoustic night to be held on a Sunday evening, A perfect way to unwind after a week of rock n roll.

She went for the idea, and soon after 'The Acoustic Sessions' began.

The original flyer for the 'Acoustic Session'

Interior pics of Oscars featuring Alec and his Screaming Nighthawks band. The stage area was below the raised bar area, offering an excellent view.

It was a bit of a risk, but on opening night a small trickle of curious punters soon grew and by the end of the night it was packed.

What's more important, there were quite a few very good musicians turn up, a lot from the quality bands who played there out to do their party pieces.

Alec had been keen to re-kindle the acoustic ethic found at his Cloggies venture 20 or so years previously...i.e.true folk music would be welcome, but overall there was literally an 'anything goes' policy.

Within a few months it was clear it was a successful formula, with musicians coming to play from all over the northwest playing a variety of styles and genres.. Blues, rock, folk, original, covers and just the plain bizarre.

Leon Afon, one of the original performers at Oscars Acoustic Sessions

The standard was pretty high and some of the sessions were put out on a cassette recording called 'Anybody Got A Capo?'... a title Alec resurrected as the name of his radio show dedicated to the open mic scene, and, at time of writing, currently available on YRLS radio and BluesRadio.UK as well as Mixcloud and the like..

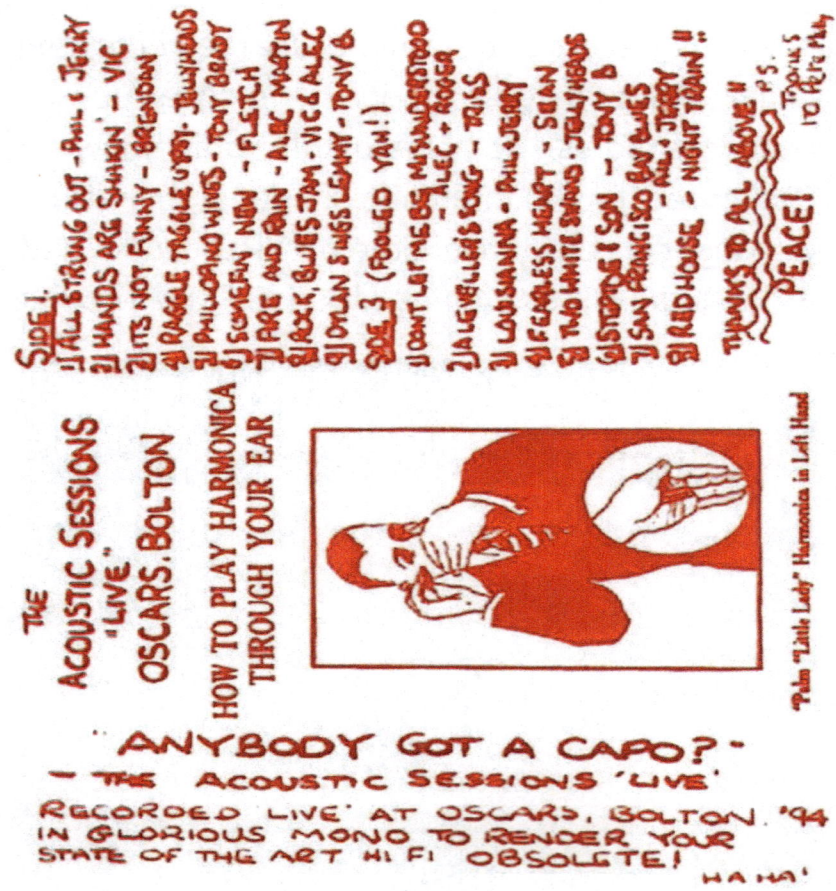

The original, hand made cassette sleeve of the Acoustic Sessions 'Best' of compilation tape made by Alec in 1994. Extremely rare!

After a year or so, another pub approached them to put on a similar night, this time mid week. Alec didn't want to use the name 'Acoustic Sessions' though.

He'd always been a fan of the Pete Brown album 'Things may come and things may go, but the Art School Ball goes on Forever"... and thus the name Buskers Ball was coined, a name he still uses to this day.

For a couple of years, the two open mics ran together, the Buskers Ball taking place on a Tuesday night in a friendly down to earth pub called the White Lion, meanwhile over at Oscars things were going from strength to strength.

The Acoustic Sessions were invited to take part in the massive Bolton Shows held on Leverhulme Park, which attracted crowds of hundreds of thousands to the town. They played two years running. The first in glorious weather, whilst the second year was in torrential rain. There was so much mud, the Army;s display of tanks couldn't function, but still The Buskers Ball soldiered on!

Indeed comedian Sir Ken Dodd was seen in the audience, prior to his show that night in the Albert Halls.

Alec and his partner Margot also put together several annual North West Songwriting Competitions which attracted entrants from all over the country, and had celebrity judges such as Clint Boon from the Inspiral Carpets to judge the live performances.

Dave Rowley, winner of the very first North West Songwriting Competition at Oscars, organised by the Buskers Ball.

The North West Songwriting Competitions were held annually for 4 or 5 years and consisted of a series of a dozen or so heats, with a grand final.

The competition attracted more than 100 entries from all over the UK and was recognized and listed by the influential International Guild of Songwriters.

So as to be seen scrupulously fair, each heat had a panel of 3 judges comprising various celebrities with, in addition to Clint, BBC presenter Alan Beswick (who admitted to knowing nothing about music), some actors from a couple 'soaps', and Bolton's very own Bob Williamson and Bernard Wrigley among others.

Some of it was filmed by Granada TV, and the BBC also picked up on it.
Prizes included recording time at a couple of top studios and music gear from the town's music shops.

Winners of the first 4 competitions were local musicians Dave Rowley, Phil Roberts, and Kirsty Mcgee taking the honours, alongside Linda Jennings who was runner up.

This indicated the quality of singer/songwriters in the area, with the Buskers Ball playing its part in their development.

Oscars chief Gay Nuttall was quoted in the local paper:

"The great thing about this competition is that absolutely anyone could enter it. The judges were looking for originality, melody and lyrical content, and it was a great success"

Not so successful though was one particular entrant who came up that day on the train from Bristol His song 'Fireman Pete' was an almost exact copy of the 'Postman Pat' theme and that was immediately spotted by the bemused judges and crowd.

After performing it, he returned home, no doubt with his tail between his legs, and not waiting for the result!

The Jellyheads at Bolton Show

The Busker Ball 'AllStars' with Chris Driver and Cpt. Ron

Janet Mather at Bolton Show

Bolton Show crowd

the very first 'Buskers Ball'

Alec performing the very first song at the very first 'open mic' in the UK

Margot having a fag whilst singing

The crowning glory: Alec and Margot were able to secure a business loan for a proper CD compilation of all the regular performers.
Using local recording studios, around a dozen or so Bolton based artists were sent off to record one or two original songs to feature on the album 'Out of Oblivion'.

The album was actually premiered at Oscars, played through the sound system, although this nearly didn't happen as no-one remembered to bring a CD player, but one was eventually found.

A cold Sunday morning at Bolton Town Hall

None of the artists had heard the others tracks, and after each song a spontaneous round of applause erupted.

It got rave reviews in the Big Issue and other magazines, and all the players were invited to perform the whole album together at Manchester's 'In the City' festival.

Despite now being well over 20 years old, the album still sounds fresh, and seems to have got something of a cult status in Japan of all places, where used copies of the limited edition sampler seem to go for silly money.

The original test pressing

Kev Bates & Stella at White Lion

Nat Clare, much admired songwriter who wrote to the local paper suggesting Bolton should erect a statue of Alec. His plea was ignored.

One gripe about the CD (and this is a warning to anyone else thinking of doing something similar), after borrowing the £5000 needed to finance the venture, paying for whatever studio time was needed, paying for artwork, registering with PRS, and having 1000 copies produced by a major CD printer, plus the hours of time spent organising the whole thing, it was expected the featured artists would at least make some effort to promote it - to their friends at least.

But no!

We had given each artist a complimentary copy, and were shocked to hear of some people on it actually taping and duplicating the CD to give to their friends.

Disappointing to say the least!

Another blow was that 400 copies were placed in the local Virgin Megastore, and lost forever when the store shut for good a few weeks later. Its these CDs that can regularly be seen for sale by bankrupt stock retailers on the internet.

NEVER AGAIN!

In the end, the White Lion got sold and converted to flats.

Oscars too changed hands and was converted to a 'ladies only' gym, despite the fruitless attempts by a Buskers Ball consortium to buy the place and retain it as a music venue.

And thus ended a glorious chapter in Bolton's music history.

Then the Buskers Ball moved, to an Irish themed pub on the opposite side of town called Dirty Nellys.

Run on a Saturday afternoon from 4pm till 9pm ish, at its peak it was the only place in town worth going.

The place was jam packed and on a couple of occasions even attracted members of the England Rugby League squad.

Musicians and performers were queuing up to play, and even by 5pm the atmosphere was as buzzing as some pubs only get late on Saturday nights.

The rest of town was deserted.

'Broken Heroes' playing Bolton Buskers Festival - Alec, Margot and Tony

Alec was once stopped in Blackpool whilst playing with his band, by a couple who asked him who was 'that guy in Bolton who ran an open mic on a Saturday afternoon?'

When Alec said it was him, they replied 'they were bloody great times, thanks!'

Indeed at its peak, they were bloody great times, but what a lot of people failed to appreciate, were the weeks before it took off, when a couple of musicians were playing to just a handful of audience (mainly disinterested drunks).

The place began to get even more packed (too packed in fact), but the atmosphere changed over the years it ran.

It was becoming more a place to meet and get legless, rather than a place to listen the music.

Performers were beginning to take it for granted that they would get a good response, and several had become jaded and repetitive.

To add to this, several new performers, already nervous at playing to such a large audience, were beginning to feel intimidated.

The throng had mainly come to hear the regular musicians, and payed scant attention to any newbie that was there to play music that actually required listening to.

Indeed one poor guy was pelted off stage with beer mats.

And now I have come to a point I will be making later in the book about 'rooms'.

A new venue was opening up just around the corner, literally a 100 yard walk away. All good things
come to an end (even The Beatles split up!), and after 4 years or so it was decided that the Buskers Ball at Dirty Nelly's had become a bit of a monster.

The new venue asked if the Buskers Ball would like to move to their place (it was actually called The Place) and given the situation the organisers agreed.

It was a large venue, with stage and lights, and the new owners couldn't have been more enthusiastic about the venture, organising a lavish opening night with free champagne and food.

They had hoped most of the musicians would move with them to the new venue, and indeed on the opening day several did. But they just didn't like it, citing quality of beer, seats, and bar staff as a reason for not going.

It was even said that it was too far out of the town centre (even though it was literally just 100 yards down the road).

They tried their best to compete with the old venue, where a couple of regular performers had jumped in straight away, more or less stabbing them in them back, when they were trying for a better venue.

They tried booking top bands as guest artists (one was a well known American artist who had come touring the UK and whom we were very lucky to get Apparently he'd heard of the reputation of the Buskers Ball and was keen to play!).

No matter how they tried though, people just wouldn't go, and the few who did just came to mock, act stupid or even just wreck the afternoon. In many ways, the old venue had become a bigger attraction than the music that was being put on.

The lunatics had indeed taken over the asylum and frankly couldn't do the job.

The Ice Band playing at The Place, Bolton

Shortly after the closure of The Place, they packed in the running of the original venue, leaving Bolton, which had at one time been the centre of the open mic scene, without any open mic for a period.

Following the disappointing end to the Dirty Nelly's saga, Alec abandoned the Buskers Ball to concentrate his effort into his blues band, Night Train.

This was, in reality, a blessing in disguise, as he composed, and then got the band to record their first album 'The Silence Spoke' a highly regarded and well reviewed concept album, based loosely on his experiences as a young rocker in an area dubbed the 'Lancashire coalfields'.

Night Train then and now..can you tell which is which?

Alec fronting his band Night Train

It wasn't long however till the Buskers Ball was resurrected.

The landlady of a reasonably upmarket village pub in Egerton asked Alec to take the sessions up there.

The pub was called The Cross Guns situated right up on the moors between Bolton and Blackburn and had a resident ghost.

A little hesitant at first, due to Alec not knowing if anybody would actually turn up to such a remote spot, Alec was swayed by the offer of free b&b after the gig.

And so started a long run of very enjoyable sessions.

Opening night was a little nervy due to the location (and the presence of Lizzy, the resident ghost), but bang on opening time the hourly bus from Bolton arrived, pretty full, and deposited a host of musicians and music followers on the doorstep.

Fifteen minutes later a second bus arrived from Blackburn and brought a whole load more.

Coupled with a large number of curious villagers, the place was buzzing, and the music went on 'til the early hours, with even more people arriving during the course of the night by car and taxi.

Alec looks back on this time with great fondness, and remembers the standard of music was equal to, if not higher, than that at Oscars 10 years earlier, and certainly higher than that had been found at Dirty Nelly's.

Younger artists who hadn't been attracted to the chaos of the latter days at Dirty Nelly's began to appear, and they were good!

It was here that Alec first met an extremely young Danny Jones and his sister Vicky who performed as a talented duo Y2K. Danny of course went on to join McFly (against Alec's advice!).

Alec and young Danny, could have been contenders! Or Alec could have joined McFly

It was also here that a BBC employee recorded a couple of sessions using top quality equipment. The results were staggeringly good, and it was the re-discovery of these minidiscs that prompted Alec to begin his 'Anybody Got a Capo' radio shows.

(Incidentally it was **also** here that Alec did in fact seethe ghost of 'Lizzie', believed to be that of Lizzie Rushton who wandered through the pub to her murder on the moors in the 19th century. There were several other witnesses too)

As can be heard on the recordings, the younger fresh-faced performers had brought an infectious enthusiasm to the Buskers Ball.

For the older more experienced musicians, it meant they had to up their game, and the friendly rivalry between youth and experience produced some great nights (a lot of great nights in fact) as can be heard on the near faultless recordings.

There was still a lot of drinking and partying going on, but the oppressive 'drink culture' that permeated Dirty Nelly's towards the end was suddenly replaced by a dedication to the quality of music.

Mick Harrington at the Brass Cat, Bolton

It was during the Cross Guns era that there was news of a Bob Dylan concert at Stirling Castle in Scotland. Quite a few of the regulars decided to go up, as Alec had arranged a Buskers Ball there during the afternoon for the travelling fans.

These were the days of the Newsgroups on the Web, and somehow Alec had acquired Bob Dylan's email address.

He sent a message to Bob inviting him to come to the afternoon session on the promise of a pint of Guinness but thought no more about it.

The session was at The Best Bar None in Stirling centre, and was pretty packed. Half way through Alec's set the crowd hushed and stood up. Alec turned round to look through the large windows, and there, in a stretch limo with the windows wound down, was the man himself.

He tipped his hat, wound up the window and was driven off, leaving Alec to ponder just what he would have said to him.

The popularity of the Cross Guns prompted the 3 or 4 neighbouring pubs to want an open mic of their own, which Alec agreed to do on different nights.

At one point, he was running six a week, and even the full McFly band showed up at one of them to celebrate Danny's birthday.
No pictures exist though.

And this is where over exposure (mentioned elsewhere in the book) comes in.

There simply wasn't enough enthusiasm (or money) for people to come to every one, and looking back, Alec realised his mistake of doing too many in a small area.

Attendances at all the venues were watered down, with the once mighty Cross Guns also taking a hit.

And so it was decided to halt the over saturation of the area completely, and all Buskers Balls in the area were abandoned

Gaz Drury, one of the exciting younger musicians that graced the Cross Guns

For a while, Alec again concentrated on his band, but also organised a series of Buskers Balls with varying degrees of success in other areas. The Lostock Arms, The Beaumont, The Briarfield, The Mop, The Hulton Arms, The Swan, Elements, Molloys, The Cattle Market, Ancient Shepherd, Downtown and Last Orders in Hindley to name a few, all hosted sessions at some point.

The next lengthy lengthy run of Buskers Balls however was at a new town centre venue called Northern Monkey.

This was a brand new bar/micro brewery with enthusiastic owners, and ran for few couple of successful years, interrupted by the dreaded Covid.

Alec has fond memories of Northern Monkey, even though the seats were particularly painful this was negated by some particularly fine (and strong) real ales.

Many of the people who had appeared at earlier events turned up, and most of the time it was standing room only!

It could get a bit noisy as the crowd from the local Wetherspoons wandered in, but they soon realised what was going on.

When Margot and Alec finally got married, they even held their reception there, with an all day open mic where many top musicians performed from all over the area !

One of the stand-out performances was by Amanda Jayne Haywood, who sang the Etta James classic,'At Last' ... very apt lyrics!

And now we learn of the value of promotion by the venue!

Things went wrong at the end of 2022 when the owner rang Alec as to why attendances were dropping (a fact that hadn't gone un-noticed).

Alec had been doing the usual publicity drops but the new bar manager hadn't been mentioning the sessions on the bar's web pages. There was a direct correlation between the two and serves to remind us that publicity by the venue is just as important as that by the organiser.

At Northern Monkey there were no posters up, and even the solitary A-frame at the door was removed.

Build and they will come.... but they need to know about it first!

Shame really cos during the time at NM The Buskers Ball had been invited to have a stage at the award winning Bolton Food and Drink Festival two years running (although if the first was like Woodstock, the second was more like Altamont!)

Bolton Food n Drink Festival

In the couple of years before Covid, Alec had also undertaken Buskers Ball events at The Old Market Tavern, Altrincham and Lucky 8's Rock n Blues Bar in Chorley, and both are rock venues.

The break for Covid didn't seem to affect them much, and all the regulars returned to carry on with the music... Altrincham being on the first Sunday of the month, and Lucky 8s being on the second.

Whilst both are rock pubs, the OMT is a massive rambling old pub, whilst Lucky 8's is much like a terraced cottage, but both have a great atmosphere and attract quality musicians.
Both are still running after many years!

Alec was keen to have another regular session in Bolton though as a base. The Buskers Ball. was after all, still technically called the rather grand 'The Buskers Ball of Bolton, England'.

With the town being midway between Altrincham and Chorley, Bolton was indeed the melting pot so to speak, where players from the other two Balls could meet up and play.

And it was good that musicians from Altrincham could meet their Chorley counterparts, and vice versa.

At the time of writing, Alec has found a new promising Bolton venue, the newly re-opened Prince Bill in the town centre, which will host the Buskers Ball on the last Sunday of the month.

Anthony Rowlands at The Prince Billy

Phil Lloyd at the Prince Billy

Incidentally, many people wonder how Alec became involved with his radio shows?

From a very early age Alec was well into blues music, and bought his first album by Howling Wolf at the age of eleven when most of his friends were more into Lulu, Sandie Shaw and Chicory Tip.

An opportunity arose when Greater Manchester Rock Radio wanted a blues presenter. Alec applied and was snapped up, and began his program 'Have I Got Blues For You'. A couple of years later though he got the opportunity to move to the more prestigious Blues Radio UK which had several ex BBC presenters, including Roxy Perry and Richard Dunning.

Alec also suggested a program about the open mic scene, called 'Anybody Got a Capo' and to his surprise the station agreed. The show features a lot of 'live' recordings from all over the UK, and is unique in being the only show on the station not to feature some kind of blues.

And so Alec currently hosts both 'Have I Got Blues For You' and 'Anybody Got a Capo' on both Blues Radio UK and YRLS.com, and actively seeks contributions of material from the open mic fraternity.

"Can't wait for Alec Martin book comes out - for those that don't know Alec - he is the godfather of open mic nights and has been running them around the North west for the over 4 decades

He is writing a book about his life on the road - I first met him at Oscars bar in Bolton probably 1996 at 19 yr old and I'll never forget our first conversation
Alec: so why do you play guitar?
Leon: so I can meet girls

Alec then proceeds to introduce me as Leo who plays guitar just to meet girls"

Leo Afon

The Gallery

Just a few, a very few, photo's of the musicians that have played the Buskers Ball.

Rick Brooks (bluesman)

One of the girls Leon Afon hoped to meet

Toria Rose Wooff

Holly Jenkinson at Downtown

Nick and Phil wish they hadn't started this jig

Irish dancers waiting to get up and Riverdance

Stu Warburton toasts the audience... Cheers Stu!

Indeed it was

Crazy Horse tells his Shirley Bassey tale

Mark Moloney tells tales of Liverpool

Ian Aspinall looking to get recognised from Corrie

Nat Clare wishes he had a statue in Bolton

Psychedelic Sid at the Joiners, Chorley

Karl Stanley didn't think he'd be in this book

Stringbox make it to Altrincham

Paul Gee wonders why he keeps getting asked to do Space Oddity

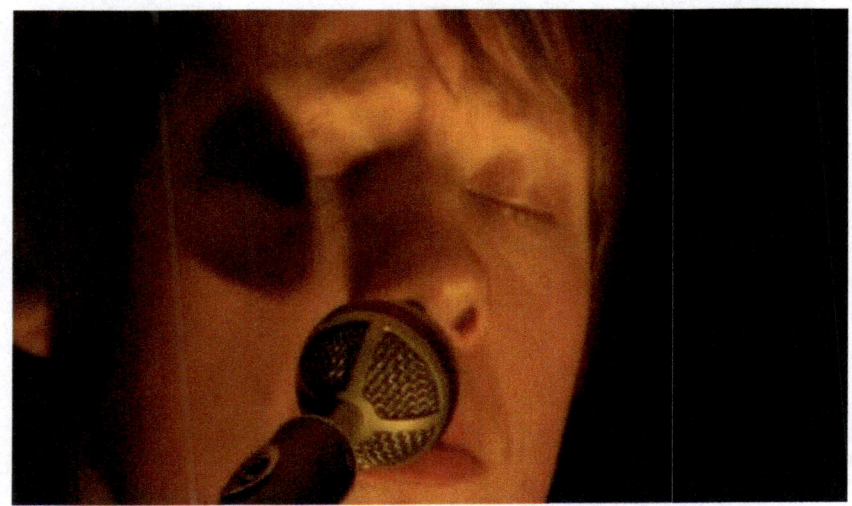

Gaz Drury sniffs the microphone

Dave Hull at Prince Billy's

James Bimson

Amanda Jayne Heywood auditions for The Who

Karl Stanley can't believe he's in here twice

Buckles Maguire

Shaun Lomax and co

Dorrie Welton helps dad out

Matthew Burtenshaw wishes he had long hair

He has now!

Mike Welton and the Marketeers

Tony Walsh asks 'How long have I got?'

It was a long time coming...

So Amanda sings 'At Last'

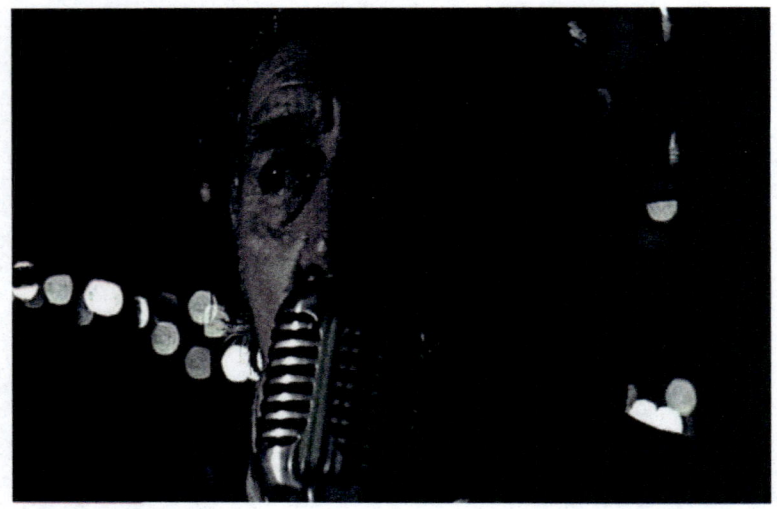

Bob Pender

Graham Farrell gets in the Xmas spirit

Trident at The Beaumont

Joy and Jake

Wagontown

David O'Keefe at Hale Barns

Wiz Moseley at Bar Metro

Phil Roberts

Pete Tate at Downtown

Thirty Minutes from Hell. Very young metal band. Probably youngest we've had on

Ash Mandrake

Lynn Jellyhead

Lewis Chapman Barker

Orpheus and the Rainbow at Bar Metro

Ryan Lennon (full name won't fit on here)

Lauren Groves yearns for a little puppy

Clive Churchward and Paula from Brazil

Kev Creamer searches for the lost chord

Ste Fletcher designer of the first Buskers Ball logo

Eternal Lovers at Bolton Food n Drink

Dr Ade Fabiola

TV Jones at The Briarfield

Inside Lees Live Lounge... very Bohemian

Dave Norris

Captain Cash performing Pastie & Peas

Steve Leech

Banjo Pete at Northern Monkey Brewery Tap

Pieter Egriega

Victor Vortex

Zak Heaney from Ideal Forgery

Susan Stanley and Rick Brooks (Mojo Rising)

Susan Stanley

Alec Martin and Pete Methy after 45 years on the road

Jim Boyer

Clive Churchward solo

Houghton Weaver Jim Berry at The Beaumont

Robert George Fox

I.T.M.A.

Dave Norris

Eric McLaren

The Happy Hippies

All My Ghosts

Masters of the Scene

Darren Wilson R.I.P.

Ben Ward

David Hanners

Tony Brady

Katie S

Nail Em Down

String Theory

Ray Spencer

Ruth Baruch

Sebastian Groves

Dog Tales

The Zimmermen

The Baby Buskers

Paul Blackburn R.I.P

Austin Mortimer

Dawn and Tania and Mike Welton

penned material on harp, fiddle, hurdy-gurdy, gaitas (Galician bagpipes) and flute.

The Weekend convinced me that small 'theme' weekends have a great future. Here we had a great family feeling plus the odd session that had a very academic feel to it. Domestically, the food was great (hurray!) and there wasn't a bar (boo!). The crunch would come if you tried to make it bigger or you stuck with a base venue of this size.

My brother, a total non-folkie, who was there for half the weekend summed it up really, "Great this, does everybody really know each other?" No, it just felt like that sort of weekend. Long may they continue.

Mike Boston

CLOGGIES The Old Man & Scythe, Bolton

As a travelling man by profession, your correspondent enjoys nothing more than a quick flip through the pristine pages of a fresh Folk Roots to see where the old guitar and harmonica case can take him, anonymous and unannounced, this month. So it was with a high degree of anticipation that I cruised quietly into balmy old Bolton which, according to F.R., sports no less than two regular folk clubs under the evocative soubriquet, 'Cloggies'.

From the pavement the wonderful Old Man & Scythe pub, built in 1636, oozes with traditional promise; ah, yes; there'll be some fine old finger-in-the-ear stuff here, no doubt.

Admitted, my visit did clash with a football match.

And it was only 8 o'clock . . .

Bombed out in one corner a bedenimmed refugee from Glastonbury snoozed deeply, his conscious hand still clutching his ganja tin. There were three others in the room, listening rapturously to repeated slabs of high-decibel Fleetwood Mac and Springsteen through a small, single-column PA system. Folk club?

"Oh, aye, yiss!" explains another bedenimmed headbanger; "Aye – it's folk club allreet – fills up a bit later on, 'bout nine . . . they all go in t'pub next door till then – beer's crap in 'ere . . ."

A few more did wander in; I was billed with a great flourish as "Our very special artiste from . . . Grimsby!" by Cloggie's supremo and organiser, Alec Martin.

Now get this straight – Cloggies does not fall into the musical or mental bracket of 'Folk Club' in any way. You have to be several wet sheets to the wind to enjoy this. For instance, in the middle of Bonny Ship The Diamond the acoustic mike was hijacked by the club's irrepressible harmonica player, John Morris, so that I had to change mid-verse from the frozen wastes of the Greenland fisheries to Chicago's South Side. Whaling waters to Muddy Waters; I lurched from shanty man to Hoochie Coochie Man in ten breathtaking seconds.

They like the blues at Cloggies, although judging by the incessant talking during each of my carefully-selected Willie Dixon compositions, no-one ever really gets to hear it. Even Alec Martin, not a bad performer at all, has a job to get through.

The night was rounded off with my hastily-assembled medley of Holly/Lee Lewis/Presley numbers where I was joined (once more against my will) by an earsplitting guitarist on an out-of-tune Stratocaster copy for a finale which had all the subtlety of a flying breezeblock.

I made a mistake tonight when I wandered into another pub called The Man & Scythe in nearby Kearsley, looking for Cloggies. The mistake was in not staying there.

"Well . . . " said one blueser, ears still bleeding, "we 'ave a laff in 'ere – don't 'ave any o' them blokes gerrin' up wi' fiddles 'n all that stuff . . . don't like that stuff in 'ere . . ."

Makes you wonder . . .

Not for the timid!

Roy Bainton

MAGGIE HOLLAND & CHRIS COE Great Western Folk Club, Exeter

A strange feature of this venue is the noise from the skittle-alley downstairs – an ominous rumbling, punctuated by outbreaks of cheering (like the backing track on Joni Mitchell's Jungle Line).

A review of Alec's Cloggies night in Folk Roots

RUNNING AN OPEN MIC

Well, you've read the story of the Buskers Ball so far, and there are many anecdotes and stories that I left out (maybe for a revised edition some time in the future).

What I'd like to do though in the remaining part of this book, is to provide any advice I can, to help those thinking of starting an open mic, or indeed may currently be hosting one (indeed for performers too!).

None of this is set in stone though, and obviously different people will have their own way of doing things, depending on personality, aims and budget.

It is though a collection of various hints and tips I would have found useful had I known from the start.

Think of it as a 'Open Mic for dummies'

Jimmy Padraic adds an Irish touch

As A Performer

First of all, I'm assuming you have all actually been to an open mic at some point at least, and its encouraged you to start your own.
But what I'd like to do now is just set a few guidelines for all performers.

Its a few hints and tips, basically to establish some kind of etiquette that if followed, could make the whole open mic experience a whole lot easier for performers and organisers. Of course its up to you if you follow them or not.

A simple couple of phone calls could save you a wasted journey, with all the disappointment and expense that that brings.

Also bear in mind that if you message the venue via social media, they may not reply straight away as they are busy running the place and can't attend their screens. Stick to a phone call for certainty.

A phone call to the organiser is also beneficial as its a way to tell him you are actually going and to reserve a spot for you. Organisers are always uncertain as to how many will be turning up, so they'll appreciate your call.

Whilst on the subject, its really bad etiquette to say a few weeks before that you will be attending and then just not show up.

Again a phone call or text message is all it takes. I often get these early confirmations, and if no-shows happen week in week out from the same people I just ignore them eventually and write them off as time wasters.

Right, you've made it to the venue so there are two things you can do. Either walk straight in with your instrument and announce yourself, or leave your instrument in the car, go in, and keep quiet while you assess the place.

I've done both, so its up to you. All I can say as a performer is, there is a certain plus point in just wandering in without an instrument and checking the place out. Not all open mics are the same.

Have a look at the PA, listen to the first couple of songs, check the audience out. Just get the feel of the place if you don't have the confidence to go striding in.

There was a reason for that.

Speaking of etiquette, it really bad form to leave straight after doing your spot. OK you may have performed cringe worthily bad and not even received a single clap, creeping off stage with your tail between your legs, but you should still stay the course of the evening (although if you have to go early, its better to announce that before you even start playing).

Everyone else in the room has listened to you, so its just the decent thing to stay and listen them.

You may even pick up some tips or receive advice!

Another definite no-no is to leave immediately after eating any free buffet that's been offered, unless its made you feel sick!

At one open mic I ran, the food was so good even the audience used to just appear when the buffet was announced, and likewise disappear as soon as they'd scoffed it.

Takeaways in that area of town did very little business on open mic day, and couldn't work out why.

Very well let's turn our attention to your actual performance. Clearly your song choice is entirely your own, and music of any style or genre is usually welcomed.

If its your first time at the venue though and you are planning to do a set of original material, remember the audience won't have seen you before and won't know what to expect.

As a host and performer I would always recommend opening with a cover of a song an audience will know, that reflects your style. If they don't like anything else they may appreciate that.

I once knew a girl in her early 20's who told me she'd written over a thousand songs. I asked if she had written over a thousand good songs, as there is a difference.

I may have upset her, but its worth pointing out that even the greatest modern songwriter of all time, Bob Dylan, had only written maybe 800 songs (and indeed not all of them were good) and that was over a period of sixty years.

Its hard to for an audience to listen to original music in a standard open mic environment. There are too many distractions to concentrate fully on what the artist is trying to convey.

Even the high calibre performing songwriters would be hard pushed to retain an audience's attention if their concert consisted entirely of unheard brand new material, All of them refer the audience to something they are familiar with at some point in their shows.
Even Bob Dylan!

In no way am I denigrating anyone who performs their own material by the way. As someone who records very open mic I run, I take great pleasure in listening the 'original' artists' tracks when I get in. Its a much fuller experience.

All I am saying is mix your original material with at least one or two covers. It works.

Of course once you've played the same place a couple of times, the audience will be familiar with your work, and you'll be able to introduce more and more of your own songs as you've developed a rapport.

Trust me on this!

Once you open the Doors/Choosing a Venue

Playing to an empty room can be heart breaking, but just remember that person coming through the door is a potential regular.

Acknowledge their presence, maybe say hello, and try your best to make him want to stay and even come back with a host of friends.

Musicians and open mic 'followers' are more likely to be drawn to a venue with a quaint (or trendy) name such as 'Ye Olde Woolpack' rather than 'Stans Sports Bar'.

One important point to bear in mind when choosing a venue, is anywhere appertaining to being a 'sports bar' is generally best avoided, for a couple of reasons.

Firstly, it's highly unlikely that any of the bar's regular clientele would be enamoured or appreciative of their games of pool, or nights watching the big match on to interfered with by a bunch of troubadours warbling and strumming away (however good,).

There is always the risk too that any really big sporting event could result in the open mic being canceled altogether, or delayed till after the match (particularly galling if the match goes into penalties or the boxing match needs a decision on points).

Bear in mind that it's not too cool either if performers turn up to find all the pub's giant screens on full volume, to be greeted by screams of 'GOAL!' as soon as they walk through the door.

In general, sport and music just don't mix... and if there is a clash, sport will always win out.

An example of this is an open mic I ran several years ago, named Lees Live Lounge.
It was virtually tailor-made for a successful open mic event.

Persian rugs on stage, quirky hippy artifacts on the walls, and luscious low lighting.

The sumptuously decadent room at Lees Live Lounge

A selection of the free food available!

To cap it all, the landlord's daughter in law provided the most delicious free food for everyone.

This wasn't just a slice of Aldi pizza, it was gourmet style meals with all the trimmings and sauces. The kind of food a trendy gastro pub would charge a fortune for.

But could we get anyone in?

No.

I ran the evening for just over 12 months, but despite it being such a great room (I could have lived there!) it was with great regret that the enthusiastic landlord and myself came to the conclusion it just wasn't working, so we called it a day.

Since then, I have talked about it to several people on the open mic scene, and though they'd heard of the event, they never went.

When asked why, they replied 'Because we thought it was a cabaret venue'

One huge advantage for a successful open mic is to hold it in a venue that already has band nights at weekend.

Established music venues will already have a dedicated music loving clientele, and whilst they may be more appreciative of Bruce Dicconson than Bert Jansch, well, it's all rock n roll to me, and many are prepared to give it a go.

In one of these venues I was working in, I was approached by a huge giant of a guy, biker with a Pantera t-shirt.

He asked if anybody could do a spot and I said yeh, More to placate him than anything.

To my surprise he turned up the week after with a keyboard, and proceeded to play some exquisite piano tracks by Beethoven and Debussy…to a completely silenced and gob smacked audience.

Just goes to show, don't judge people on their appearance.

Chris Grindley plays Debussy at Lucky 8's

Trevor Croft

In a town centre pub, learn to identify your potential audience. Clearly if someone turns up with a guitar strapped to their back, chances are they have come to perform. It's important though to actually make contact.

Remember if it's their first time in that particular pub, they may feel awkward but chances are they'll feel a certain amount of nervousness too.

Just introduce yourself , ask their names... you'll need to know it if you're planning introducing them on stage.

There's nothing worse than an introduction along the lines of 'Ladies and gentlemen, can we have a round of applause for...erm...erm'.

Danny Kinsella

Other things you may like to ask are what kind of material they do (I've always liked to separate similar type artists e.g. if someone is likely to perform Oasis covers, don't have someone else following straight on who does the same material, stick someone who does originals in between.)

Also just ask where they're from and how they found about this event.

The former will give you additional material for the introduction, whilst the latter can tell you if your publicity is working.

Did they read about it on Facebook? If so, which group. Did they just see a poster or did someone suggest them going?

It's all good information that will help you concentrate your publicity… and not only that, it will make you feel good to know that a particular poster in a music shop window was worth putting up, or that a post in a certain Facebook group worked.

Lauren Groves celebrating completing a song!

Phil Seddon and Nick Panting wishing they hadn't started one

All You Need Is Love

Before you begin running an open mic, there's one question you really want to ask yourself...
'Do you really wanna do it?'

Although in theory it sounds great, and may provide you with a little pocket money, but there are a couple of things to bear in mind,

Firstly, a successful open mic is a long term commitment.

You'll need to be prepared to go to the same venue every single week.

There'll be times when it's snowing, torrential rain etc when you simply don't feel like driving or setting up. But that's just tough.

If you don't turn up, not only will you be letting the venue down (and remember they may very well have booked extra bar staff) but you'll also be letting down your audience and the (hopefully) half a dozen or so musicians who have braved the elements.

There is nothing worse for a performer than turning up at a venue with a couple of guitars, walking into the pub, and being told there's nothing on because the host hasn't shown up. Then to sheepishly walk back out.

Although an enterprising confident musician may well reply 'well if you've nothing on, do you fancy an acoustic session whilst I'm here?'...
it has been known to work.

Steve Bridges R.I.P. at The Mop

As I said earlier, due to the fleeting nature of some open mics, it's always advisable to telephone the venue before setting out to make sure it's still running. There will be several gig listings on social media for open mics in your
area, but these aren't 100% reliable. Even if the open mic is mentioned the day before, it's still advisable to check on the day. Any events first announced 3 months or more ago should always be checked out.

People who are keen to advertise their sessions when they start are less enthusiastic about removing their posts when they stop. Some open mic organisers still leave their old posts on when they have changed venues, so beware.

The Impromptunes at Northern Monkey Tap

Googling open mics in your area will bring up dozens of results, but many of these will be out-dated. Of course the best way to discover open mics is word of mouth.

Another 'beware' issue is probably something you never imagined, and that is 'over exposure', as happened to me and is mentioned in part one

If you have an open mic that runs weekly for a year, that's 52 mini shows you'll be required to do... to largely the same regular audience.

Open mic hosts are generally expected to open the night, performing half a dozen or so tunes before the first of the night's troubadours take the stage

If you are lucky you'll have enough performers to fill the entire session... if you are lucky!

Chances are though, there'll be some unexpected non arrivals, especially if it's bad weather or something really good on tv.

Strange people at the Brass Cat

This means technically you could be doing 52 actual gigs at the same venue.

Sounds fun, but don't expect any other venue to offer you a paid guest spot, when people can see you playing once a week down your local boozer!

A good friend of mine from my Black Lion Days Steve Munnoch

Having only a couple of guests isn't good

You can usually extend the playing times to cover these situations, however the chances are you'll have to fill in with a few more tunes. And should the unthinkable happen and no other guest singers... well you've got an audience to entertain for the night so make sure you have learned enough material for any eventuality.

Looking on the bright side, your session may very well be over subscribed. Although whilst it's good to have lots of performers it can be problematic.

Rob Pusey and Linda Jennings

Alec Martin and Roger Bridge

Derek Workman flexing his powerful voice

Robert George Fox with Bose PA columns

It's always a good idea when advertising on social media, to ask people who want to play to message you to book a spot.

This helps you in as much as it gives you an idea as to numbers, but it's also reassuring for them to know there's a definite spot awaiting them (especially reassuring if they are travelling any distance).

If you are flooded with performers, it's pretty sacrosanct that people who booked a spot in advance get to play a decent spot.

This also applies to people who turn up right at the start of the evening, and it's also a good idea to get these people on early.

If, as the evening progresses, more singers roll up than you can reasonably fit in, you may have to ask singers waiting to come on to cut their set, e.g. if you have told them four song maximum, cut them to three.

It's generally not good form to turn performers away, they may think it's been a waste of time attending and not bother coming again, and worse still, they may tell their friends

"I went to such and such a place, and they wouldn't let me on".

Not a good look for your event!

This brings us to an important point when organising an open mic. When asked, as you will be, 'how many shall I do?'. I've always found it better to answer in terms of time.

Six performers in a three hour session works out at 30 mins each, but (and it's a big but) factor in the changeover times.

Depending on the experience of the artist, this could be as little as a minute. Straight on, tuned up, plugged in and go!

On the other hand, a beginner may arrive onstage with guitar untuned, a huge pile of lyric sheets for which he requires a music stand, he may request a stool and indeed his instrument may require a microphone.

His guitar strap may need adjusting, he may need the vocal mic placing in front of his mouth... he may even ask for a capo!

All this takes time, and if his 5 song repertoire consists of 5 minute songs, then that's gonna throw out the timing for the rest of the night's schedule, especially if he hasn't actually planned a set and spends minutes wading through his lyric sheets to just pick them out.

I was once playing an open mic where the organiser came up to me and told me I'd be on after the singer who was on at the moment and he'd be doing two more songs.

I dutifully prepared myself mentally, got my guitar out of its case, tuned up, and decided what I wanted to do.

The guy who was on finished his penultimate song, a three minute ditty (I'd gone out of the room to tune up so not to disturb him) but he then proceeded to announce his final song would be Dylan's 'Desolation Row' which clocks in at over 11 minutes on the album.

Surely I thought, he won't be doing the full length version?

He did.

But worse than that, he was reciting the words from some kind of songbook, where he actually stopped playing to turn the page every couple of verses or so.

Not only that, but he kept making mistakes musically, mis-fingering chords, and each time he insisted on starting the verse again!

Now I'm a huge Dylan fan, but I swear that particular version must have lasted 30 minutes. All with me psyched up and waiting to go on.

Worse still, the organiser asked me to cut my performance down to one song as they were running out of time.

It was all good hearted and apologetic, and running an open mic myself I knew the situation, but I'd travelled a fair way to perform what turned out to be just one song.

I'm certainly in no rush to return there.

Whilst I'm on this subject, two things to be wary of:

First of all, beware anyone who has had a few, got Dutch courage and asks if he can 'have a go' and then asks to borrow your guitar! Unless I'm really desperate to fill time my reply is usually, no.

It's better to do this politely and make some excuse along the lines of 'my guitar is not in standard tuning', or 'the battery has gone'. It usually does the trick!

Monologue Joe... no guitar needed

Another type of performer who may ask to have a go, is someone who uses a backing track from their phone.

To be honest I've found these people ok, and some really rather good.
It just depends really which direction you want to take your open mic.

In the spirit of a true 'open mic' I usually agree and put them on as the final artist, pointing out that it's just a one off. The last thing you want is to turn your eclectic open mic into a karaoke session.

Like I said, some are really good singers but if you really don't want to go down that route, then just apologise profusely (you don't want to upset their feelings) and just say you don't have the correct lead for their phone.
They can be persistent though, some will even have their own leads, so best to play it by ear.

Incidentally, isn't it always the case that these singers always introduce 'Make You Feel my Love' as being by Adele... shame on you!!!

The intensity of Phil Middleton at Northern Monkey

Alicia Jayne Harrison R.I.P.

The type of performer that is just a damn nuisance is the one that turns up regularly minutes before you are about to turn the power off!

I had one of these at an open mic I used to run. I always aim to finish an open mic session with my strongest performer.

At the end of the day they will be the one that people remember most, and if they are good they'll entice the audience back next week.

Week in week out, this guy would appear expecting to play, just as I was wrapping up.

For a time I didn't like to refuse as he was always pretty keen, and as far as I knew he may well have been working until late.

Trouble is, he wasn't exactly that competent. He'd ask to borrow my guitar and proceed with frankly painful versions of Streets of London and Country Roads.

Neither was particularly high on my list of favourite songs, but his stopping and starting whilst he looked for a chord removed any enjoyment I (or the audience) may have had.

I put up with this for quite a few months until one day I was speaking to the organiser of another open mic, and he told me of a character he dubbed Midnight Paul.
Turns out it was the same guy.

Next time he appeared at my session I put my foot down and had to tell him unless he came early in future he wouldn't get on.

He didn't take it too well, and spent years complaining and bad-mouthing me...

But there are times when you've just got to put your foot down!

Meera Ram at Xmas time

Luke Harber... top guy!

For the most part though you'll meet some great musicians when running an open mic. There's a real sense of camaraderie and I met some of my best friends at these sessions.

It's like a family...there may be rows like in any family, but at the end of the day, well, we're all in it together...

> IT'S AMAZING THE NUMBER OF GREAT PEOPLE IN MY LIFE THAT I WOULDN'T HAVE EVER MET IF IT WASN'T FOR MUSIC

EQUIPMENT

The original, and indeed some current, folk clubs didn't really rely on any technology.

All they needed was an upstairs room in a pub and a handful of enthusiastic musicians and that was it.

Indeed some really hard core folk clubs didn't even use or need instruments at all. Guitars whilst not exactly frowned on, were considered a necessary evil (with nylon strung guitars thought to have a more authentic tone over steel).

Instruments of choice were often accordions, concertinas, banjos, fiddles and possibly some sort of percussion.

I often refer to such people as 'the finger-in-ear' brigade

I remember once being asked to stand in for a presenter on a BBC Radio Folk Programme

A few weeks before I thought I'd actually better check it out to see what it was like, and was horrified to find it was a more or less 100% 'finger-in-ear' show.

My days in the early trad folk clubs had left me a smattering of knowledge of this of type music, i.e. I could actually tell my Cecil Sharpe and Ewan MacColl from my Wild Willie Barrett. I was slightly hesitant about doing it though. Should I pander to their regular listeners?

I thought no, this is my show I'll do it my way.

I didn't really endear myself to the listeners from the start of my very first track, The Incredible String Band's 'Maya' merging into Roy Harper's 'The Highway Song'.

Almost straight away the phone lines lit up complaining about my selections, and telling the 'powers that be' to "Get him off!"

The 'Finger-in-ear' brigade had struck And they hadn't even heard me speak yet!'

I digress... back to PA's.

In the early 70s though, no doubt as a consequence of the 60s beat boom, audiences expected a louder, fuller sound, and PA systems began to appear in
folk clubs. This wasn't meant to circumvent the unwritten rule of silence whilst the singer is on, audiences remained quiet.

Along with the other unwritten rule of no going to the bar or toilet when the performers on, traditional folk clubs were quite a good place for a singer to be actually heard.

The PA set up at Northern Monkey

The early club PA systems weren't that good for the most part, serving mainly as sound reinforcement for vocalists who still liked to belt their songs out 'pure voice' style.

Instruments didn't really need to be amplified as banjos, accordions, and pipes are plenty loud enough on their own.

The early 70s brought about a huge revival in folk-rock music however, and audiences began to increase dramatically due to the emergence of top bands such as the phenomenal Fairport Convention, Steeleye Span (who both had top 40 singles), The Incredible String Band and a whole host of homegrown and American singer songwriters.

BBC TV even featured bands like Liverpool's Spinners and US singer-songwriter Julie Felix (who had an amazing array of folk artists as special guests on her show) as part of their mainstream programming.

Even Leonard Cohen and the wonderful ISB if I remember correctly.

Folk clubs began to upgrade their PA systems as audiences increased, recreating the kind of sound that could be heard on vinyl and big concerts.

The main problem though was amplifying an acoustic guitar.

Up to the late 70s, acoustic pickups were pretty dire and the only way to amplify the true sound of an acoustic guitar was via a good microphone.

A couple of companies (notably Epiphone with what is now known as their Lennon model) produced guitars with built-in magnetic pickups, but these were really only used in the context of bands...for the folk club scene they were much of a no-no.

A couple of manufacturers manufactured similar devices that clipped into the sound hole and had rudimentary volume/tone controls.

Feedback was a problem, and again if you were aiming to get the true sound of your Martin D28 with one, you'd be sorely disappointed.

There was another type of pickup...a contact mic that you stuck to the guitar body.

These were immensely fiddly and needed a lot of experimentation in placing them in just the right spot to get anywhere near decent sound.

To top it all they had a habit of coming unstuck and falling off.

No, playing in front of a microphone was generally considered the only way to go, even with its disadvantages.

A true folkie's weapon of choice,

Around 1973 however, a new manufacturer, Ovation, popped up with a newly designed pickup that was revolutionary.

These were built into the bridge, and had a passive preamp and virtually made the more traditional guitar makers products obsolete. With an Ovation you could just plug in and play, rather
than mess around standing in front of microphones.

Of course the traditional big company guitars still had a following, but the unconventional Ovations with their large 'bowl' backs (reputedly made of the same material used to coat the war heads of nuclear missiles) were highly desirable. Not only that, they sounded pretty good.

Big drawback was the actual price, which put them well out of range of the average 'folkie'.

Incidentally the 1973 designed Ovation pickup is still used in the majority of Ovation guitars today. Only the preamp has changed, with active preamps now being standard.

Is that traditional enough?

The author with his pair of Ovation guitars

Early models were almost impossible to play whilst sat down.

Just under 10 years after the initial Ovations came out, another game changer appeared on the scene, courtesy of the Japanese guitar manufacturer Takamine.

These were traditional all wood dreadnought and jumbo guitars with their own piezo pickups and absolutely stunning active preamps.

To this day I still remember the first time I heard someone play a Takamine... it just blew me away.

These days Ovation copies are numerous and relatively cheap. Most sound good, but none can replicate the quality of a genuine Ovation.

Likewise there are dozens of brands that incorporate a Takamine 'type' pickup up.

It's probably harder to buy a guitar without some kind of pickup these days, unless you go for a boutique, hand made guitar .

So that's it, if you are a guitar based organiser of an open mic, just make sure you have a decent guitar with an active pickup system.

An onboard preamp preferably with built in tuner will save you countless journeys to the mixing desk to adjust the sound.

To reiterate a point made earlier though, there will be times when someone asks to play with your guitar.

This could be when they turn up with a guitar that can't be plugged in, or maybe someone who just wandered into the venue not knowing there was a music session on, and just feel like doing a song or two.

There is no hard and fast rule here, it's entirely up to you.

Its a bit of a risk though. You may not know their playing style for a start. They could break a string or really dig their finger nails into the wooden top causing scratches that instantly devalue your precious instrument.

They may even drop it!!

Best thing to do is just ask what songs they are going to do. If it's material by Jimi Hendrix or Pete Townsend, then you may be taking a risk!

Likewise with Death Metal or Punk

A bit of cajon banging

Dr David Sands

I must admit I've lent my Lowden out a couple of times, but it is stressful wondering if the guy, or gal, has a tin of lighter fuel in his, or her, pocket.

The solution is to take a cheaper second guitar with you. With this you'll have no real qualms about lending it out and whoever is playing it will probably find the experience so unpleasant, they'll remember to bring his own next time.

A spare guitar is also quite useful to have around should you break a string.

It's my contention that an acoustic player should never break a string (with the possible exceptions of energetic flamenco players).

If the strings are so old they could snap at anytime then they won't sound good and should be replaced before it happen.

If the worst does happen whilst in mid flow, it's just so much easier (and quicker) to swap guitars.

There's not much worse for an audience than to sit there twiddling their thumbs whilst the artist struggles to change a string.

It may give them a welcome opportunity to nip out for a cig... but you run the risk of them not actually coming back in!

Mick Markow and Alec at The Man & Schyte

PA EQUIPMENT

PA equipment has improved dramatically over the last few years, both in terms of quality and, more importantly for some, portability.

There was a time when 'big means best', and indeed 'old skool rockers' still believe that to this day!

Its not true of course. Not unless you are putting on a large out door event, and that's not really open mic territory.

Years ago you;d need horns,tops, mids, bass bins(and maybe even a 'sub') to fill even a decent size concert room with enough sound.

These days with improved speaker efficiency, digital amplification, and iPad type mixers its a different ball game, making a roadies life a lot easier.

Not of course that you are going to need all that for an open mic in a pub, where the majority of performers will be solo with just an acoustic guitar.

The basic essentials are a pair of powered speakers, a mixer, some speaker stands, cables, microphones and stand, and a good pair of ears.

Lighting is a plus, mainly to focus the attention of the audience on the performer.

A lot of pubs these days will have some kind of lights over the stage area, but avoid shining lights directly into the artists eyes, especially if they are using lyric sheets.

And no need to overdo it. I still hark back to the early days of the Black Lion and Cloggies, where a single white spotlight shining down on to the performer created a superb atmosphere.

Remember its an open mic, not a dance event.

Starting off with a mixer, it's always tempting when deciding which one to buy to pick the one with most sliders and knobs.

Let's face it, they look really cool especially on the sales videos where they show flashing LEDs and mortised faders moving rapidly up and down in test mode.

Don't get hypnotized!
Mixers come in many sizes and can handle inputs of 4: 8, 12, 16, 32, and 64 ... some even more!

What you'll have to do is work out how many you'll realistically need. A vocalist with a guitar will usually need 2 channels. Therefore a duo will need four.

You made need an additional microphone input to mic a cajon or double bass whatever up.

In fact its quite a good idea to take a cajon along, hours of fun for the restless.

In my experience, an eight channel mixer is more than enough for an open mic, although 12 may be useful if you plan on using the mixer for recording at home.

Each channel will have a line input for guitar and a mic input.

Most will have reverb and most will have aux ins and outs in the form of RCA sockets.

It's not the purpose of this book to explain how your mixer works.

Best bet is to read the manual, and if are a total novice, take it with you.

You never know when you may press a button by mistake, and a physical copy of the manual is both informative as to your mistakes, and reassuring to have just in case.

MICROPHONES

Going on the old hifi adage 'Garbage In, Garbage Out' (which refers to the fact that a poor quality input source can never be compensated for in the next parts of the chain) it's important to get the best possible mic you can afford for the main vocal mic.

It's commonly suggested that Shure SM58s are some of the best mics out there, and are industry standard.

Undoubtedly they are popular, but that's because over the years a hell of a lot have been made and sold due to lack of competition and a healthy advertising budget.

They are useful, and well thought of (mainly by 'old skool' rockers), but there are plenty better vocal mics out there.

To illustrate this, if you go to a concert or see a singer on TV, chances are they won't be using a SM58 any more.

The best mics for detailed subtle, quality vocals are without doubt condenser mics.

These will more than likely need phantom power, but don't worry this is available at the push of a button on virtually all modern mixers.

Old skool rockers will claim they aren't as rugged as they rely on internal electronic circuitry, but believe me this isn't the case.

Anyway, no open mic singer is likely to twirl the mic round his head like Roger Daltrey. And even if they did, there's no reason to think it would fare any worse.

Shure make a range of condenser microphones , but also definitely check out brands such as Beyer, Sennheiser, AKG, Audix and Earthworks.

If you're feeling flush, check out the exquisite Neumann range of hand held mics.

Old skool rocker in action.. Kev Creamer

Toria Rose Wooff using a Neumann

A good microphone can last a lifetime. It can be your best friend or choose badly and it's your worst enemy.

Best bet is to actually go into a shop and try a few. Choose the one that suits your voice...and definitely avoid any pertaining to be karaoke.

Likewise any mic, or indeed any PA gear that has the word Pro in its name usually isn't a piece of pro gear.

A couple of notable exceptions to this are a couple of Mackie mixers and I'm sure I remember Beyer making a really good microphone a few years ago. With the name Prostar, or something similar.

Anyway good luck, there's a lot to choose from and there seem to be new ones every day appearing from China (And some of these are really rather good)

By and large you get what you pay for, but remember

'Buy cheap, Buy twice

Old skool rockers will tell you the best speakers will be 15 inch loudspeakers, with horns, housed in marine ply cabinets, matching sub-woofers and monitors, powered by massive, heat producing power amps.

Erm...pay no attention.

As stated earlier, speaker technology has come a long way in a short period of time.

The ubiquitous 1x12" speaker with built in hf unit seems to be the most widely used speaker for an open mic, although a 1x10" may be acceptable.

Anything less and you run the risk of losing bass response, and anything more e.g 15" risks losing fine acoustic detail (Plus the larger speakers are disproportionately heavier)

If you're short of cash though, the s/h market is full of the older style cabinets that require a power amp, or a powered mixing desk and can be purchased relatively cheaply. Make sure to haggle.

Your bank manager will thank you, although your back won't.

Frater Rodderz (bluesman)

If it's your first sound system, setting one up can be an exciting project, certainly for the first few times.

Whilst setting up may be fun, I always found dismantling at the end of the night to be a pain and a chore.

You may wish to hurry to make sure the eagerly awaited kebab shop is still open, but if it's been a good night you'll probably be surrounded by people congratulating you (and old skool rockers reminiscing about the size of the speakers they used to carry, but they won't offer to give you a lift!)

No, these days the way to go is with a pair of easily carried and easy to pack away plastic powered cabinets with a built in 1000w amplifier, although you could feasibly drop down to 500w.

Whilst on the subject of packing up, always try to pack the cables away as they were when you bought them. An as yet unknown law of physics states that otherwise, when you come to get them out again you'll be spending hours unravelling some of the weirdest knots known to man.

Just a note, these power ratings are RMS. Many of the cheaper manufacturers will boast amplifiers of a remarkable 2000w, but that is because they measure the power differently. They are measuring peak power, not RMS.

As far as actual loudness is concerned, a 500w can produce as much, if not more, volume than a 1000w version.

The reason for this is the physical efficiency of the loudspeaker.

This will be shown in the specification sheet as sound pressure level (or SPL). A good working measurement for this is between 128 and 131db.

Always check the SPL figure.

Cheaper powered speakers that boast an astronomical number of watts will invariably be paired with cheaper speaker units that produce SPL measurements of 104db or less, and that really is really inadequate.

JBL, Yamaha, RCF, DB, Mackie and Yamaha are the names to look out for, To be honest you won't really go wrong with any of their speakers.

Check out too for ultra portability the systems that consist of two speakers clipped to the body of the mixer amp, usually the size of a small suitcase. Peavey, Fender and Yamaha make these kind of units.
Fender's is called a Passport.

In my experience the sound quality does not match the larger alternatives, but they can be handy at certain venues, and are always even handier as a spare back-up system.

Check the reverb on these units, as some of them skimp on the quality to cut costs, and a bad reverb sounds dreadful, as does a ping pong style echo.

The price difference in their ranges will reflect the tone and audio quality, but for an open mic, even the cheapest of their range should be more than adequate.

An unusual development in the PA department was the introduction of the column system by Bose quite a few years ago.

Users of these systems tend to swear by them (well they have to, considering the financial outlay) and many claim that just one is adequate.

As a former owner , I can confirm that just one is just that, adequate. That's just a personal view of course.

I moved on to buy a pair, and the sound quality improved, but to my ears they just didn't produce a decent sound stage.

The quality was almost hifi like, but somehow the imaging let them down.

Another disadvantage with the Bose column system was the actually transporting and setting up.

Each side had four separate units that required setting up. An amplifier section, a bass unit and two sections of the column.

With two columns, that's 8 separate pieces that require assembling (and indeed disassembling).

Since Bose, several other manufacturers have introduced similar 'line array' systems, so the best performers bet is to try them out (and bear in mind the transportation/assembly issues).

To mind mind though they are very much the emperors new clothes. They look really cool and sound good but for just an open mic, to me at least, they are overkill.

I'm certainly glad I reverted back to a conventional system, although a lot of solo performers are more than happy to use them. Having said that though, there are an awful lot of used units on the s/h market.

Whilst on the subject of speakers, you may wish to consider some kind of monitor system so the artist can hear themselves properly.

These aren't strictly necessary, and performers don't usually expect them, but if your open mic is prone to noisy audiences, they are a nice touch.

Rather than a wedge speaker on the floor, a couple of manufacturers now offer small units that attach to the mic stand.

I found these quite useful if you can cope with any potential feedback issues.

Certainly worth considering.

It's always useful to have a few bits and bobs. Probably the most useful implement is a capo.

Whilst you personally may not use one, many people do, but it's surprising how many people neglect or forget to bring their own.

Bear in mind it's always worth having a couple of these, as, like plectrums, they have a habit of disappearing

Always carry a spare set of strings, maybe a spare microphone, and a music stand plus maybe an attachment that can be clipped to a mic stand to hold an iPad or phone.

Whilst many performers don't need 'prompts', many do.

PUBLICITY

The value of publicity can't be stressed enough!

With so many open mic sessions opening and closing the choice for musicians (and audiences) to play somewhere and listen music is overwhelming.

Thing is, you want them to come to yours!

In the first instance social media seems the obvious choice.
A colourful post on Facebook for example may seem enough, but bear in mind other open mics will also have their posts up too.

In the open mic groups found on FB there are dozens of open mics vying for attention, and a poster put on one of them may soon slip down the listings.

A good idea is to create your own group, and invite

It will also create a sense of 'community' and people who meet at the actual open mic can 'friend' each other (if they wish).

If your open mic does close, it's also important to announce this, as the last thing people want is to turn up somewhere to be told the open mic stopped months ago.

It's also a good idea to keep group members involved in some way.

Post pictures and videos for example, ask them for comments and plead with them to share content.

A 'like' for example, takes no effort at all, yet can help when the great FB algorithm is working out material to display to other groups.

In my opinion, despite all the social media advantages, there's no real substitute for a paper poster stuck on the wall in the venue itself, plus a few stuck up in local music shops etc.

I once held an open mic in a pub on one of the busiest roads in the country, the A6.

Not only that, it was at a crossroads with traffic lights. Thousands of people were stopped looking at the pub every day, waiting for the lights to change.

Yet the pub had no outdoor advertising!

I pointed this out to the manager, and got him to do an A Frame outside.

The week after we got quite a few more people attending, including one guy who lived 50 miles away but passed the pub every day on his way to work, but never knew there was anything on there!

Happy Hippy Nige

The Opening Night!!

OK, you've found your venue, decided on a start date, done the publicity, got the gear, and prepared yourself mentally.

The big day has arrived!

First thing to do is get to the venue early!

Loading your stuff in may be relatively easy, but bear in mind there may be difficulty parking.

Also remember, the actual layout of the room may need rearranging, and more than likely you are the one that will need to do the shifting.

They may for example have been serving food and the room is set up for that, or they may have expected you to set up in a small corner that isn't suitable.

Remember, this is your night as much as the pub's, so be firm and try to negotiate the best possible stage area.

Max did it his way

A spot of culture at an open air Buskers Ball

Alec on the big stage at Hale Barns Carnival

Another reason to get there early, especially if its your first time is to avoid making mistakes with the equipment.

It could be you have forgotten the mixer, or some other vital piece of equipment, in which case you'll have to make a quick journey back home.
It could be you have damaged a cable, indeed many things could go wrong. This is why its useful to take manuals with you so you can refer to them.

Once set up, actually test how it sounds. Get someone to speak or shout into the microphones and adjust volume levels etc.
There will be times during the course of the evening that you need to adjust volumes (depending on the voice of whoever is singing) but its always important to get that basic setting right.

And try not to have wires trailing all over the place!

and no non-players near the stage

Ok, unless you are extremely unlucky (the weather is atrocious or there's a world cup final on TV) you should now get people and musicians filtering in.

As stated before, engage with all of them.

Make them actually feel welcome.

For some people, coming to an open mic can be as daunting as actually organizing one.

I'm often reminded of one particular performer who was so nervous when she got up, my girlfriend, Margot, had to hold her hand. She was literally shaking!!

Since then, this singer actually moved to Nashville where she recorded a couple of great albums and received accolades from none other than Bob Harries (of Old Grey Whistle Test fame)
so bear in mind the old devil of nerves.

Just a note, as people are settling down, its always a good idea to play some background music. Music that is sympathetic to the open mic theme.
Its no good playing Metallica or Pantera... keep it acoustic based.

The late John Smith, a true journeyman musician

Having fun in Cheshire

More fun in Chorley

Introduce each artist as the night progresses with "will you welcome onstage xxx" May sound a bit corny, but it creates an atmosphere, and at least whoever is performing will have had a round of applause at the beginning of their spot (if not the end!).

A point I have missed is deciding the running order. I've seen places that have a chalk board showing vacant slots. This is an excellent idea because it means early arrivals can choose when they want to go on. Late arrivals are just stuck with whatever slots are available. It works well!

Otherwise use your discretion, but remember, always try and end on a strong artist. Its what the audience will remember as they drift home.

At the end of the proceedings, before you start packing up, thank the audience for coming, tell them you hope to see them again next week (or whenever) and ask for one last round of applause for all the artists who have performed.

Again, sounds corny, but it works!!

Stuart Warburton says Goodnight

Pack up and go home to your best friend the cat

OK, you're home now, and pondering the night's events, with adrenalin flowing through your brain.

With any luck, its been a hugely successful evening, overflowing with performers and people watching intensely.

OR

Its been a tad disappointing with just you playing all night to a handful of disinterested drunks.

If its the former, don't get cocky. Not everyone will have enjoyed it (its amazing how much alcohol affects people's perceptions on the night) and numbers may be down the second week.

If its the latter, well you did your best but don't give up!

Open Mic's are notoriously fickle as to numbers attending.
A highly successful evening one week may very well be followed by a complete drought the following week[1]

A lot of performers like to spread themselves around to as many open mics as possible.

The 'new Ed Sheerhan' who wowed your audience one week may not return to your event for several weeks, but all things being well, and you haven't upset him, then chances are he will be back at some point in the future as its now on his radar.

Similarly a quiet opening event doesn't mean that more people won't come in the future.

The sustainability of an open mic can't be judged by the first couple of weeks.

My opinion is it takes at least a couple of months to get established.

And its important to stress this to the landlord or manager of the pub. The first few weeks may see the number of attendees fluctuate wildly.

A few landlords think of an open mic as a quick fix for an ailing pub, cheap entertainment that will bring people in, but the reality is an open mic may take several hard months to establish itself

If, after a few months, there's no sign of improvement, then its best to admit it hasn't worked and call it a day...

No hard feelings either way, and be careful not to burn your bridges with the landlord. You may well meet again down the road if he ever takes up a different pub!

Don't give up though, even though you may be devastated.

Reasons for failure are many, and sometimes unfathomable.

Try again somewhere else.

There are hundreds of potential venues out there who would welcome an open mic, and as their popularity grows so does the demand.

What doesn't work at one venue, may very well be a roaring success at another, even if its next door. to quote Kate Bush...

Don't give up!!!!

THE BUSKERS BALL ROLL OF HONOUR

Over the last 5 decades, countless musicians have turned up to play The Buskers Ball (some even tuned up!)

The overwhelming majority seemed to enjoy the experience, (although there were a couple of miserable sods)

So may I say a BIG personal THANK YOU to all the people on this list, although I know there are many many more I may have missed.

Its an age thing!!!!

Margot Martin, Pete Farrow, Mary Asquith,
Karl Stanley, Rick Brooks, Susan Stanley
Robin Lipson, Jessica Lyon Wall,
George Borowski, Brent Mason, Fat Badger,
Lauren Groves, Robert George Fox,
Eric McLaren, Trevor Croft, Sebastian Groves,
Ben Ward, Chris Grindley, Chris Driver, Triss,
Clive Churchward, Mike Welton, Dorrie Welton,
TheDeansgate 3, Lauren Groves, Pete and Chrissy Clarke,
David Gordon, Shaun and Sarah Lomax, Mark Summerfield,
Dave Hull, Matt Finn, Jimmy Padraic, Mark Lowey, LLoyd Rhodes, Matthew Darwin, The Marketeers,
The Jellyheads, Gaz Drury, Danny Jones,
Vikki Jones, McFly, Nick Jackson,
Darren Poyzer, Phil Middleton, Rachel Appleton,
Paul Crompton, Ste Fletcher, Tony Brady, Vic Gilmore,
Tony Backhouse, Sugar Stealers, Adrian Mortimer,
Jim Boyer, Kev Bates, Danny Kinsella,
Nick Panting, Phil Middleton, All My Ghosts,
Michelle Cowlishaw, Nial McFadden, Bob Williamson,
The Happy Hippies, Helen Walker, Different World,
Theresa Darbyshire, The Kookaburras,
Steve Parker Jones, Stewart Farqharson, David Gordon,
String Driven Thing, Keith Bateson Stringbox,
Janie & Paul Britton, Amanda Jayne Heywood, Zac Heaney,
Mick Markow, Keith the Fiddler, Steve Munnoch, Pat Martin,
Trevor Hyett, Captain Cash, John McFadden,

Graham Farrell, North By North West, Alcatraz Blues Band,
Paul Waterworth Joanne Holt, Johnny Shock, PhilMahon,
Gerry O'Laughlin, Stu Warburton, Psychedelic Sid, Jim Sax,
Roger Bridge, Phil Lloyd, Lee Richards, Tony Walsh, Tony
Rowlands, Shells Bells, Cold Flame, Kirsty McGee, Dave
Rowley, Bob Pender, Roydan Styles, Ideal Forgery, Ted
Edwards, Ricker George, Alchemist and Blacksmith, Rebec,
Graham Davies, Nat Clare, Paul Blackburn, Dave Morgan,
Mick Hayes, Ste Leech, Orpheus and the Rainbow,
Mick Harrington, John Smith, The Cakes, Tom Walsh,
Linda Jennings, The Guthrie Boys, Janet Mather,
Paul Anderson, Lee Harrison, Tony Walsh, Hovis Presley
James Ashcroft, Jack Coogan,, John McLoughlin, John Barlass,
Cider Ouse Entourage, Derek Austin,
Derek Workman, Trilogy, Captain Ronnie, Joan Blackburn,
Monologue Joe, Graham Clark, Frater Roderz, Paul Gee,
Cold Flame, Steve Wood, The Aquaphibians, Colin Liptrot,
Tony Devlin, Lynne Collier, Rosie and Barry Hardman,
Barry Lee, Charlotte Peters, Andrea Glass, Anne Davies,
Deborah Markwick. Waiting4Bob, Intermittent Signal,
Paul Gastall, Chris Driver,   Paula Gaspar, Ruth Baruch,
Ken Jackson, Leon Arfon, Mark Summerfield, Clint Boone,
Gay Nuttall, Lee Baylis, Dave Sands, Ade Fabola,
Uke Punk, Nicki Jay, Andy Stones,
Eternal Lovers, Stu Butterworth, Scotch Malc, Ray Spencer,
Dave Norris, George Whittle, Sean Blunt, Amy Corcoran,
Ken Jackson, Lewis Chapman Barker, Ashley Sherlock,
Adam Swarbrick, Ryan Lennon, Rob Young, Max Burns,
Kev Creamer, Me and Im, Alicia Jayne Harrison,
Toria Rose Wooff, Pieter Egriega, Wagontown,
Paul Meagher, Damian Skellhorn, Holly Jenkinson, Jan Marie,
David O'Keefe, Keith Sloane, Optical Bus Stop,
Ruth Everson, Voodoo Dolls,
Jan Jay, Victor Vortex, Meera Ram, Ian Aspinall,
Lee O'Shaughnessy, Barry Livesey, David Hanners,
Masters of the Scene, Phil Seddon, Leon Arfon,
Ste Bridges, Martin Stimson, David Hull, James Bimson,
Colin Liptrot, Dan Lever, Dave Lomax,
Tony Wardle, Badly Drawn Boy, Tony Rea, Triss, Ian Brown,
Starsailor, Banjo Pete, Rob Pusey, Alan Houldsworth,
Martin Gittins, Pint n Half, John Norris,
The Baby Buskers of Brighton,

And Bob Dylan (read the book!)

And a BIG thank you to the following venues

The Victory, Oscars, The Cattle Market, The Blue Boar, TheYork, TheMop, TheBriarfield , DirtyNelly's, The Gypsys Tent, The Man And Scythe (when it was good),The Golden Lion,The Swan, Old Isaacs, The HultonArms,The Cross Guns, Dunscar Arms, Spread Eagle, Portland,The Lostock Arms, The Beaumont, Hare and Hounds,Northern Monkey Bury Met, Bar Metro,Old MarketTavern, Q Inn, Hennighans, Molloys, The Last Orders, The Wiganer, Monteraze, Elements, Hale Barns Carnival,
The Trotters Jolly Carter, Duke of Wellington,
The Belgrave, The Railway,The Moses Gate, Downtown,The Alma, The White Lion,
Dog n Partridge, Lucky 8s Rock n Blues, Bar,
Big House Blues Bar, Ancient Shepherd, Big House Rock Bar,Prince Billy's, Bolton Food n Drink Festival, Bolton Show, Best Bar None (Stirling)

and some trendy bar in Castlefield....

AND A BIG THANK YOU TO ALL THE AUDIENCES OVER THE YEARS, WITHOUT WHOM THE OPEN MIC SCENE WOULD NOT EXIST

HOPE TO MEET YOU ALL SOMETIME

Alec Martin
December 2023

Printed in Great Britain
by Amazon